POWER PASSERS

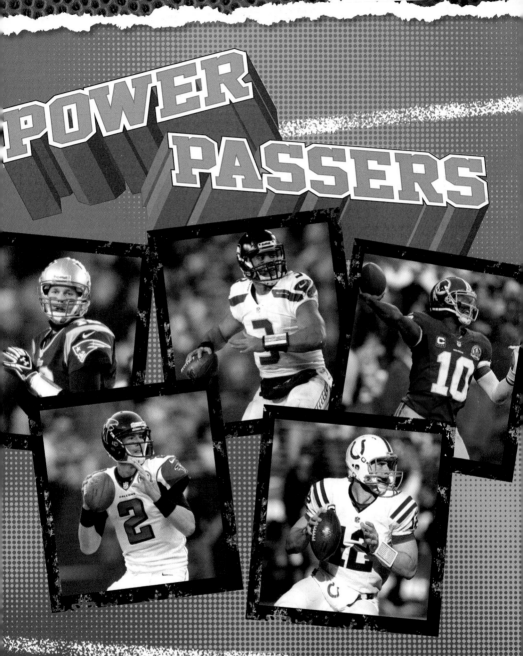

BY K. C. KELLEY

SCHOLASTIC INC.

ISBN 978-0-545-58514-9

12 11 10 9 8 7 6 5 4 3 2 1   13 14 15 16 17 18/0

Printed in the U.S.A.   40
First printing, September 2013

Designed by Cheung Tai
Photo editor: Cynthia Carris

TOM BRADY

February 3, 2002: Late in the fourth quarter of Super Bowl XXXVI, Tom Brady stood over center, looking at the St. Louis Rams' defense. His Patriots were tied with the Rams, 17–17. Just being that close in the game was a big victory for New England. The Pats were a 14-point underdog coming in. But Brady was used to being an underdog. Only a year earlier, he had spent the entire season on the bench as New England's backup quarterback. That came after being drafted way down in the sixth round.

Now the young passer had a chance to win the Super Bowl. Over the next ninety seconds and nine plays, Brady calmly ignored the screaming crowd and the intense Rams defense. He guided the Patriots into position for placekicker Adam Vinatieri to try a game-winning field goal. The kick was good, and Tom Brady was a Super Bowl champ . . . and the game's MVP!

That Super Bowl win was the start of one of the best quarterback careers in NFL history. Since taking over as the Patriots' starter early in 2001, Brady has helped the Pats win three Super Bowls. In 2007, he set a single-season record with 50 touchdown passes, and he also guided his team to ten straight seasons of ten or more wins.

Brady grew up in northern California. In college, at the University of Michigan, he was passed over for the starting job several times. Finally, as a junior, he got to lead the Wolverines, and by his senior year, he had taken them to ten wins and a victory in the Orange Bowl. Even that success did not make him an NFL lock. The Patriots had a star quarterback in Drew Bledsoe, but they took a chance on Brady in the sixth round. In his first NFL season, Brady completed exactly one pass.

But ever since Brady got his first chance in 2001—after Bledsoe was injured—he has not given up his spot. Brady and the Patriots followed their Super Bowl win with another title two years later. In Super Bowl XXXVIII, Brady and Vinatieri did it again. With the game tied late, Brady led a solid drive as the clock ticked down. He got his kicker in position to win the game—and Vinatieri delivered yet another clutch field goal. The Patriots beat the Carolina Panthers, 32–29, and Brady won his second Super Bowl MVP trophy.

The next year, Brady helped the Patriots become the seventh team ever to win back-to-back Super Bowls. He threw two touchdown passes in New England's 24–21 win over the Philadelphia Eagles.

Though Brady and the Patriots have not won the Super Bowl since (they have made it to the game twice, in Super Bowl XLII and Super Bowl XLVI, but didn't win), they have remained among the league's elite teams. For his part, Brady has continued to put up amazing numbers. He has led the NFL in touchdown passes three times and passing yards twice. He has ten seasons with 3,500 passing yards or more, including a career-high 5,235 yards in 2011 (the second-highest total of all time).

Along with his calm leadership ability, Brady has shown that he can adapt his skills to the team's needs. For the first half of his career, the Patriots were a great mix of run and pass. Brady didn't have more than 30 touchdown passes in a season until 2007. Then Patriots coach Bill Belichick took advantage of Brady and a great group of receivers to focus more on passing. Brady responded with a record 50 TD passes and has since had three more seasons with 30 or more.

Brady also showed his toughness by coming back from a terrible knee injury.

In the first game of the 2008 season, he was hit hard by a Kansas City Chiefs pass rusher. Brady crumpled to the turf and ended up missing the entire season. He came back strong in 2009 with more than 4,300 passing yards.

Among his many honors are eight Pro Bowl selections, a pair of Super Bowl MVP trophies, two AP NFL MVP awards, and the 2009 Comeback Player of the Year title.

For Patriots fans, however, the one title that Brady has earned the most often is the most important: winner.

PEYTON MANNING

October 15, 2012: As a national TV audience watched on Monday Night Football, the San Diego Chargers knocked the Denver Broncos all over the field. This was Broncos QB Peyton Manning's first season in Denver after a Hall of Fame career with the Indianapolis Colts, and he was struggling. He had even thrown a "pick six," an interception that leads to the other team scoring, that helped San Diego to a 24–0 halftime lead.

But Manning is one of football's all-time greatest leaders. As he had done for so many years, he rallied his team behind him. In the second half, he threw three TD passes and carried the Broncos to one of the biggest comebacks in NFL history. They ended up winning 35–24! But anyone who has watched this marvelous athlete should not have been surprised: Manning has been "the man" for years.

Peyton Manning grew up in New Orleans watching his father, Archie, play in the NFL for thirteen seasons. A high-school superstar, Peyton surprised many by choosing to attend the University of Tennessee. His dad had been a star at Mississippi, but Peyton picked his own path. With the Volunteers, he was outstanding, finishing second in the voting for the Heisman Trophy and leading Tennessee to the top of the national rankings.

In 1998, he was the obvious first pick in the NFL draft. The Colts chose him, and over the next thirteen seasons, Manning turned a losing team into a winner.

His first season, however, was pretty rough. He set a rookie record with 3,739 passing yards, but the Colts only won three games. He also led the NFL with 28 interceptions. Manning was determined to improve, though, and by his second season, Indianapolis was in the playoffs. It was the first of eleven times he would steer the Colts into the postseason. In fact, in Manning's thirteen years with the Colts, they failed to win ten games only twice (1998 and 2001). He made his first Pro Bowl after the 1999 season and has been named to that all-star game eleven more times.

Manning led the NFL in completions, passing yards, and TD passes in 2000, and he has since led the league in those categories several times. The NFL uses a "passer rating" to measure the success of a quarterback, and Peyton has topped the league in that category for three different seasons. With a strong, accurate arm and an ability to lead his team out of trouble, Manning is everything a

team wants in a passer. He also acts as a coach on the field. He studies his opponents and knows his own team's game plan so well that he often calls plays on the spot. The sight of Manning flapping his arms and shouting to teammates is as well-known as his fluid passing style. He directs his offense like a conductor leading a band.

Manning and the Colts were winning a lot of regular-season

games, but falling short in the playoffs. Finally, they put it all together in 2006. The Colts beat Tom Brady and the Patriots in a thrilling AFC Championship Game. Then, in Super Bowl XLI, Manning threw for two touchdowns and was named the MVP as the Colts beat the Chicago Bears, 29–17. After nine years as one of the top QBs in football, Manning was finally a champion.

He continued with Indy for four more seasons, leading them to the playoffs each time. Manning kept racking up the passing yards, too (he has topped 4,000 yards twelve times in his career, more than any other QB), and TD passes (his career total of 436 is second all-time behind Brett Favre). He played in every game the

Colts played from 1998 through 2010.

In 2011, however, that amazing streak ended. A serious neck injury forced Manning to have surgery and miss the season. Many thought he would never play again. The Colts decided to let him go in March of 2012.

Manning had other ideas. He worked nonstop to come back from the injury. He signed with the Denver Broncos to keep his amazing career going. After missing all of 2011, he rolled into 2012 without missing a beat. He had another 4,000-yard season, was third in the NFL with 37 TD passes, and led the Broncos to the best record in the AFC. In the playoffs, the Broncos lost to the Baltimore Ravens in a tense double-overtime game.

Manning's season with Denver just proved what everyone already knew: Peyton Manning is one of the two or three greatest quarterbacks ever. He is the complete package: great arm, toughness, smarts, leadership, and more.

The best expect to be the best, and Peyton Manning expects nothing less.

AARON RODGERS

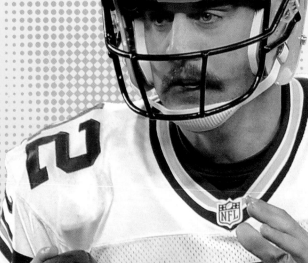

February 6, 2011: It's called the victory formation. When a team knows it has the game in hand, the quarterback takes a snap and just kneels down. On this day in Dallas, Packers QB Aaron Rodgers set his team in the victory formation. He got the ball, took a knee, and when he stood up, he was a Super Bowl champion. Rodgers had passed for three touchdowns and 304 yards in the game, but more important, he had proved himself to everyone who had doubted him. The longtime backup who was once "the guy who took Brett Favre's place" was now a champion, too.

Growing up in northern California, Aaron Rodgers was an all-around athlete, but football was his best sport. He set many records for his high-school team, while getting nearly all A's in class. After a year in junior college, Rodgers became a star passer at the University of California at Berkeley. He helped the Golden Bears win the 2004 Pac-10 title and a Holiday Bowl berth. But there were other top passers in the 2005 NFL Draft. Rodgers fell all the way to twenty-fourth overall, where the Green Bay Packers snapped him up. Rodgers's NFL dreams had come true, but over the next three seasons as a backup QB, he threw a total of just 35 passes.

Backup QBs in the NFL are sometimes called "clipboard guys." They stand on the sideline, holding a clipboard with the team's plays, and watch the starter get all the glory. If the starter is injured, the backups are thrust into the spotlight. It can be a

frustrating way to be in the NFL. For Aaron Rodgers, however, his three years as a backup helped him become the outstanding player he is today. Part of the reason is that he was backing up all-time great Brett Favre. Watching Favre game after game from the Packers' sideline, Rodgers learned a lot about being an NFL star. The other part of the reason is Rodgers's focus. He studies opponents endlessly. He goes over his own playbook until he knows it backward and forward. The seasons spent as a backup gave him time to study.

In 2008, the Packers decided he was ready to lead. They let Favre, their longtime cornerstone, go and gave the job to Rodgers. In Rodgers's first season as the starter, the team went 6–10. Fans grumbled that the Pack had made the wrong choice.

Rodgers buckled down and worked even harder. By 2009, he had led the Packers to the playoffs. By 2010, he had them playing in Super Bowl XLV. The team's big win in that game, 31–25 over the Pittsburgh Steelers, put to rest any worries fans had about losing Favre. In Rodgers, they had another winner.

As great as his 2010 season was, Rodgers and the Packers were even better in 2011. They lost only one regular-season game. They were going for two titles in a row when they were tripped up in the playoffs by the New York Giants. Then in 2012, the team struggled early, losing three of their first five games. However, Rodgers righted the ship. Green Bay lost only two more times and won the NFC North again. Rodgers was second in the NFL with 39 TD passes.

In 2011 and 2012, Rodgers led the league in passer rating. In fact, his 122.5 mark in 2011 is the all-time highest. And his 104.9 career mark is also the best ever. The rating showcases all the things that make Rodgers so successful: He is very accurate—he has averaged only eight interceptions over his five full seasons as a starter. He throws for a lot of yards—in only one season has he fallen below 4,000 yards (2010), and that year he had 3,922!

Along with his other skills, Rodgers showed a lot of patience waiting for his chance—and he has made the most of it!

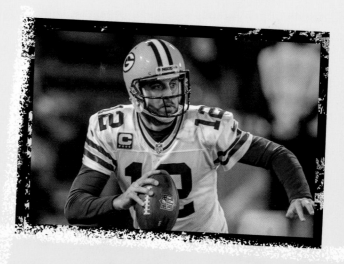

MATT RYAN

September 7, 2008: Matt Ryan felt the pressure. He was just a rookie, but he had been handed the starting quarterback job with the Atlanta Falcons. The team had won only four games the year before. This was his first game and all eyes were on him, many expecting him to fail. But he had worked too hard to reach this spot. He knew he needed quick success to get the fans on his side.

He dropped back to make his first pass in the NFL. He saw wide receiver Michael Jenkins streaking down the field. Ryan's strong arm powered a perfect throw. Jenkins caught it in stride and raced to the end zone, completing a 62-yard TD play. One pass, one TD: Ryan's career was off to a flying start!

Growing up in Pennsylvania, Matt Ryan was one of the top passers in the state. When it came time to play in college, Ryan followed the family—his uncle had been a quarterback for the Boston College Eagles. After a solid season as the BC starter in 2006, Ryan had a new head coach for his senior season. And the new coach unleashed Ryan's talents. The previous coach had favored short passes and the running game. The new coach saw Ryan's power arm and changed the offense. By midseason, the Eagles were among the best teams in the nation, rising as high as No. 2. Ryan helped by leading the team on several late, game-winning drives. He ended up breaking the school record for TD passes and was given the Johnny Unitas Golden Arm Award as the nation's top quarterback.

Coming into the 2008 NFL draft, Ryan was considered the best quarterback available. The Falcons had the third pick and chose the strong-armed young passer. They thought so much of young Ryan that they made him the starter from his first game. It was a gamble, but it proved to be the right choice.

In Ryan's rookie season, he led the Falcons to seven more wins than they had had the previous season. The team also earned its first playoff spot since 2004. Ryan threw for 3,440 yards in the season and was named the NFL Offensive Rookie of the Year. Though Atlanta did not make the playoffs in 2009, they did go 9–7. The back-to-back winning seasons were their first—even though the team has been around since 1966.

Ryan put all the lessons from his first two seasons together in 2010. He guided the Falcons to a 13–3 record, the best in the NFC. Green Bay beat Atlanta in the playoffs, but the Falcons and Ryan had established themselves among the NFL's best.

In his next two seasons, Ryan led the Falcons back to the playoffs twice. He also improved his own stats in every area—passing yards, touchdown passes, and passer rating. He led the NFL in 2012 with a 68.6 completion percentage. That last stat shows one of Ryan's biggest strengths: accuracy. He also has one of the best deep throws in the league. Ryan has had at least one pass play of 70 yards or more in every season except 2010.

In 2012, Ryan set career highs with 4,719 yards and 32 touchdown passes, while earning his second Pro Bowl selection. More important, the Falcons won the NFC South again. In the playoffs, the Falcons lost a tough matchup to the San Francisco 49ers in the NFC Championship Game, but the future looks bright for Matt Ryan and the Falcons.

COLIN
KAEPERNICK

SAN FRANCISCO
49ERS

January 12, 2012: The Packers didn't know what hit them. The mighty Green Bay defense, used to having its way with opposing quarterbacks, looked lost. Though Colin Kaepernick had only been the 49ers starting QB for eight games, he seemed like a Hall of Famer in this divisional playoff game. He went through the Packers defense for 181 rushing yards, including a game-breaking 56-yard score. His total was the highest for a quarterback in NFL history, regular or postseason. A kid who had started on the bench made his mark on history!

When Colin Kaepernick was in fourth grade, he wrote a letter about his future. He hoped that he would grow to be 6 feet 4 inches tall. He loved football, so he wrote that he wanted to be the quarterback of the 49ers when he grew up.

Guess what? Both dreams came true!

In 2012, the 6'4", second-year passer was one of the best stories in the NFL. After taking over as the 49ers' starting QB midway through the season, Kaepernick led the team to within four points of a Super Bowl championship. When his life began, however, it was hard to imagine such a terrific outcome.

Kaepernick was adopted when he was five weeks old. His birth mother lived in Milwaukee, but he joined the family of Rick and Teresa Kaepernick and their two other children. Kaepernick struggled early with illness and breathing trouble. But his parents made sure he got help and he got better fast.

The family moved from Wisconsin when he was four and made their new home in the California farming town of Turlock. It's a quiet place, and Kaepernick was an athletic star early on. He won NFL Punt, Pass & Kick contests and also used his marvelous arm as an all-star pitcher. His brother, Kyle, says his hands used to hurt after catching Kaepernick's pitches. Major League Baseball teams wanted to draft him, but Kaepernick had other ideas. He wanted to stick to football.

At the University of Nevada, Kaepernick's coaches created a game plan to take advantage of his skills. The move paid off with a stack of wins, including a huge upset of No. 3–ranked Boise State in 2010. At the end of his senior season, Nevada was ranked No. 11, the school's highest ever. Kaepernick also became the first quarterback in NCAA history to have more than 10,000 yards passing *and* 4,000 yards rushing.

The 49ers chose Kaepernick in the second round of the 2011 NFL draft. For a year and a half, he backed up Alex Smith. However, in the 49ers' eighth game of 2012, Smith went down with a concussion. Kaepernick came off the bench to lead the team to a win, but more importantly, he amazed coach Jim Harbaugh. In one of the most surprising decisions in recent years, Harbaugh

benched Smith—who was playing great—and made Kaepernick his starter.

Kaepernick energized the 49ers, making big passes and stunning runs. He led them to a pair of playoff victories. The first was a 45–31 romp over Green Bay in which he set the rushing record. The second included a playoff-record 17-point comeback over the Falcons. In Super Bowl XLVII, the kid from Turlock struggled early on. However, in the second half, he brought the Niners to within a few points. Among his big plays was a 15-yard TD run, the longest ever by a quarterback in the Super Bowl. After the run, fans got a chance to see him "Kaepernicking," the nickname for his biceps-kissing TD celebration. If not for a final goal-line stand by Baltimore, Kaepernick might have earned a Super Bowl ring.

Kaepernick has shown remarkable skills for a young player. With a winning smile and a positive attitude to go with all-world skills, the sky is the limit!

THE YEAR OF THE ROOKIE QB

The 2012 NFL season was the Year of the Rookie QB. A record five first-year passers started on the NFL's opening weekend. Three of them led their teams to the playoffs, another first. Along the way, those three each showed off their physical skills. But more important, they also each showed that they were mentally ready for the tough NFL season. Here's a brief look at three power passers that NFL fans will be watching for many years.

ANDREW LUCK
INDIANAPOLIS COLTS

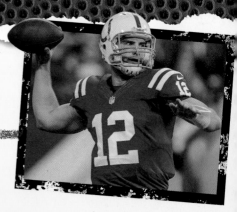

Like Peyton Manning, Andrew Luck is following in his father's footsteps. Oliver Luck played five seasons in the NFL in the 1980s. Andrew grew up watching his dad, and took the skills he learned to Stanford University. He lead them to a No. 4 national ranking in 2010 and a school-record eleven wins. After his junior season, he finished second in the Heisman Trophy voting behind future NFL rookie star Cam Newton.

Many experts felt that Luck was ready for the NFL, but he played one more year at Stanford. With a new coach, Luck improved in 2011. He was named on the All-America team and won several national player of the year awards. However, he finished second in the Heisman vote again, this time to Robert Griffin III.

In 1998, the Indianapolis Colts had made Peyton Manning their No. 1 overall pick. In 2012, they had first pick again, and they chose Luck. As great as Manning was in his first year, Luck was even better. He set a new rookie passing-yards record with a total of 4,374. He also broke Newton's single-game mark, throwing for 433 yards against the Miami Dolphins. Manning won only one game as a first-year player; Luck led the Colts to ten wins and a playoff spot.

Luck is a great passer, but perhaps his best skill is his confidence. He has the attitude of a veteran as he leads his team. Though he and the Colts lost in the first round of the playoffs, with any luck, Andrew will be back there again in 2013!

ROBERT GRIFFIN III
WASHINGTON REDSKINS

The Redskins were once among the NFL's best teams. They won two Super Bowls in the 1980s. In recent seasons, however, they had stumbled. Their last NFC East title came in 1999. They had earned only two playoff spots since then, most recently in 2007. They needed help . . . and along came RG3.

In Robert Griffin's senior season at Baylor, he burst into the national spotlight. He gave his Heisman hopes their biggest boost with a huge win over the University of Oklahoma. Tied at 38–38, with time winding down, Griffin led an 80-yard drive, hitting Terrance Williams with a 34-yard pass that gave Baylor the win.

Griffin won the Heisman, finishing ahead of Luck. When it was time for the draft, the Colts had the first pick, and they chose Luck. The Redskins were very pleased to get Griffin with the number-two overall pick.

Griffin has not disappointed. In fact, he had the lowest interception percentage in the NFL in 2012, throwing only five picks in nearly 400 pass attempts. His 102.4 passer rating was third in the league, trailing only veterans Aaron Rodgers and Peyton Manning.

In the playoffs, Griffin was hampered by a knee injury that slowed down his running game. But the first-round loss just made his desire to get back to the postseason that much stronger.

RUSSELL WILSON
Seattle Seahawks

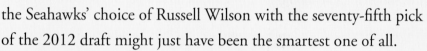

Luck and Griffin got all the attention by going at the top of the draft, but the Seahawks' choice of Russell Wilson with the seventy-fifth pick of the 2012 draft might just have been the smartest one of all.

With the Seahawks, Wilson was expected to back up newly signed Matt Flynn. In training camp, however, Wilson impressed coach Pete Carroll. The young passer showed all the skills needed to succeed: poise, a great arm, a deep knowledge of the offense, and leadership. To many people's surprise, Carroll named his rookie quarterback the starter.

Wilson had a rocky start as the Seahawks lost half of their first eight games. However, he and the team were learning to play together. In the second half of the season, the Seattle offense boomed. After throwing eight interceptions in the first half of the season, Wilson threw just two the rest of the year. He had only 10 TD passes in his first eight games, but he threw 16 in the last eight. His final total of 26 scoring passes tied Peyton Manning's single-season record for rookies.

Led by Wilson, the Seahawks went on a scoring binge to wrap up the regular season, while the Seattle defense shut down opponents. In the wild-card playoff, Wilson led the Seahawks to a win over Griffin and the Redskins. In the next round, his furious second-half comeback was nearly enough, but Atlanta and Matt Ryan rallied for a game-winning field goal.